MW00887891

YOU'RE ABOUT TO LEARN ABOUT THE PRESENT AND FUTURE OF MARKETING

Welcome!

Social Media is one of the most effective communication and advertising channels. But cutting through the noise can be challenging, and often, marketers must use paid social marketing strategies to amplify their message in social platforms.

Even though you might have created a really insightful piece of content, it can be hard to reach the right audience, especially in the beginning, where no one knows you or your brand. You can use social ads to boost your existing content, for example your Facebook posts or your blog.

Highly targeted ads on social media can help you reach exactly the people who care about your content. The ability to target potential readers and customers based on demographic data, behaviors, and very specific interests is the biggest strength of social media ads.

But social ads are not limited to promoting content; they are also a great way to advertise products, drive traffic to your website or online shop, or collect contact information for your email campaigns.

In this guide, you learn what is possible in several leading platforms and learn how to evaluate which platform is right for your message and your audience. On the next pages we cover six major social media platforms: Facebook, Instagram, Twitter, Pinterest, Snapchat, and LinkedIn. Each of these sites has more than 100 million monthly active users.

Table of Contents:

Table of Contents:

Facebook:

About Facebook:

Facebook probably doesn't need much of an introduction – launched in 2004, the social network now is the largest social media platform with more than 1.7 billion monthly active users worldwide. The company today is more than just a social network – Facebook acquired messaging app WhatsApp and started its own successful messenger. They also bought photo-sharing platform Instagram and the virtual reality company Oculus VR.

Since most Facebook users log into the site every day and engage with other users, brands and content, the platform knows a lot about their users. For advertisers Facebook is one of the most attractive online channels, because it lets them utilize their rich user data to target very specific audiences. And since most companies and brands are already present on Facebook, ads are a great way to build a following and boost engagement for the content they share.

What Facebook ads look like:

Here you have four different choices – you can create an ad that features a single image, a single video, or multiple images that are displayed either in a carousel format or as a slideshow.

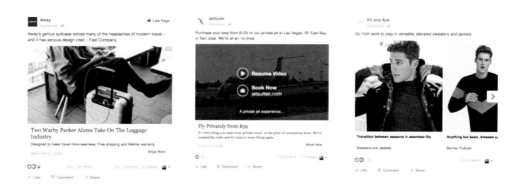

| Single Image | Single Video/Slideshow | Carousel |

Facebook:

Facebook also offers a new, more immersive ad experience on mobile. They call it Facebook Canvas. Canvas looks like a normal mobile news feed ad, but once a user taps to open the ad, he or she is taken to a full screen experience (videos, images, text, products) that the advertiser can customize.

Here is an example of how cruise company *Holland America Line* used Facebook Canvas to advertise a Caribbean getaway:

What objectives can I meet with my Facebook ads?
You can optimize ads on Facebook based on what specific objective your campaign has.
Generally, Facebook distinguishes three different kinds of objectives that follow the traditional user journey from awareness to conversion:

1. **Raising awareness:** This includes campaigns to raise brand awareness, local awareness and to maximize reach.

2. **Consideration:** These are ads that drive traffic to your website, boost the engagement of your posts, increase app downloads or video views and help you collect customer data (leads) to use in follow-up campaigns.

3. **Conversion:** These are ads that increase the conversion on your website or online shop∗, advertise specific products to users who have interacted with your shop before∗, or get people to visit your local store.

∗These campaign objectives require you to add a few lines of code to your website, which will then implement the Facebook pixel on your site.

Based on past user behavior data, Facebook will show your ad to those people in your target audience who are most likely to perform the action you want them to.

Facebook:

What targeting options does Facebook offer?
Facebook offers a variety of targeting options that you can combine to build a specific audience:

Location: Target users by country, state, city, zip code, or the area around your physical business.
Demographics: Target users by age, gender, education, and the languages they speak.
Interests: Target users by interests, based on profile information, pages, groups or content they engage with. You can choose from hundreds of categories like sports, movies, music, games, or shopping. You can also target users who like specific pages.
Behaviors: Target users based on what Facebook knows about user behavior, such as the way they shop, the phone they use, or if they plan to buy a house or a car.
Connections: Target users who like your page or app and their friends.
Custom: Target existing customers based on data (e.g., emails, phone numbers) you provide. You can also create Lookalike Audiences – people who are similar to your existing customers.

What is the minimum budget to advertise on Facebook?
When you set up your daily budget on Facebook, the minimum daily budget depends on what your ad set gets charged for.

The ad set gets charged for:	Min. Daily Budget:
Impressions	$1.00
Clicks, likes, video views, post engagement	$5.00
Offer claims, app installs and other low-frequency events	$40.00

If you want to set up a lifetime budget instead, i.e., a total budget for the duration of the campaign, your minimum budget is calculated by multiplying the minimum daily budget by the number of days the campaign lasts.

How to get started
Log into Facebook then click on "Create an Ad" to start advertising on Facebook.

Instagram:

About Instagram:

Instagram is an online and mobile social network for photo- and video-sharing with more than 500 million monthly active users worldwide. Users can share photos and videos publicly and privately on the Instagram app and through other social networking platforms such as Twitter, Tumblr or Facebook. Instagram started out with photos that were square shaped but now is open to pictures in any aspect ratio as well as videos with up to 60 seconds.

For Advertisers, Instagram is a fantastic platform to tell a company's story in a visual and engaging way. Successful campaigns do not sell products or advertise big discounts but bring a product's or brand's authentic heart and soul to life. Advertisers have to carefully balance the information and the inspiration value of their campaigns to encourage the community to like and share their ads.

Since Instagram was acquired by Facebook in 2012, the advertising platforms merged and most of the advertising and targeting options are the same for both platforms. Similar to Facebook ads, to run ads on Instagram, you'll need a Facebook Page for the brand or product you are promoting.

What ad types does Instagram offer?

Similar to what we have seen for Facebook, we can classify Instagram's ad options based on what the ads look like and what objectives they have. All Instagram ads will be placed in the user feed, both in the browser and the app version.

What Instagram ads look like

Here you have the same three choices you know from Facebook ads – you can create an ad that features a single photo, a video, or multiple photos that are displayed in a carousel format.

Single Ad

Video Ad

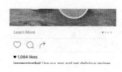

Carousel Ad

Instagram:

What objectives can I meet with my Instagram ad?

For self-service customers, Instagram offers a range of different objectives for which you can optimize your campaign. Similar to Facebook, Instagram will show your ad to the people in your target audience who are most likely to take the action you want them to take. The campaign objectives you can choose from are:

- Brand awareness
- Reach
- Traffic (for clicks to your website or to the app store page of your app)
- App installs
- Engagement (with your posts)
- Video views
- Conversions (on your website or app)⋆

⋆ This campaign objective requires you to implement the Facebook pixel code on your site. If you want to track the actions that happen inside your mobile app as a result of your ads, your developer should implement a piece of code called App Events.

What targeting options does Instagram offer?

Instagram offers the same targeting options as Facebook. You can combine them to build a specific audience:

Location: Target users by country, state, city, zip code, or the area around your physical business.

Demographics: Target users by age, gender, education, and the languages they speak.

Interests: Target users by interests, based on profile information, pages, groups or content they engage with. You can choose from hundreds of categories like sports, movies, music, games, or shopping. You can also target users who like specific pages.

Behaviors: Target users based on what Facebook knows about user behavior, such as the way they shop, the phone they use, or if they plan to buy a house or a car.

Connections: Target users who like your page or app and their friends.

Custom: Target existing customers based on data (e.g., emails, phone numbers) you provide. You can also create Lookalike Audiences – people who are similar to your existing customers.

Instagram:

What is the minimum budget to advertise on Instagram?
The minimum daily budget on Instagram is the same as for Facebook ads and depends on what your ad set gets charged for.

The ad set gets charged for:	Min. Daily Budget:
Impressions	$1.00
Clicks, likes, video views, post engagement	$5.00
Offer claims, app installs and other low-frequency events	$40.00

If you want to set up a lifetime budget instead, i.e., a total budget for the duration of the campaign, your minimum budget is calculated by multiplying the minimum daily budget by the number of days the campaign lasts.

How to get started
Instagram and Facebook use the same tool and process, via Facebook's Ad Manager, to create and manage ads on both platforms.

Twitter:

About Twitter

Twitter, also known as the "SMS of the Internet", was founded in 2006 and now has more than 300 million registered monthly active users who post and read messages with up to 140 characters. Users can add links, photos and videos to their tweets, include hashtags to help others find their message, and run polls within a tweet.

For advertisers, Twitter offers a variety of ad types that can be tailored to different campaign objectives, from increasing website visits and sales to creating a bigger following for a company's Twitter account. Twitter also offers rich options to target a specific audience, including demographic, interest and behavior targeting.

What ad types does Twitter offer?

Twitter organizes its different ad types by campaign objective: i.e., the action an advertiser wants a user to perform. Depending on which campaign objective you choose, the ad will be displayed in a different format, which Twitter calls "Cards." Here is an overview of the different campaign objectives you can choose from, and what the ads look like to the user:

Tweet engagement

Promote a new or existing tweet to your target audience. You pay for engagement with the tweet, e.g., clicks, retweets, likes, follows and replies. If you prefer to maximize brand awareness and care less about engagement, you can book an Awareness campaign. Here you pay for the number of impressions (CPM). You can attach up to four images to your tweet. If you do this, only 116 characters are available for your Tweet, as 24 characters are used for the images.

Tweet without image

Tweet with one image

Tweet with multiple images

Twitter:

Video views

Embed a video in a tweet and promote it to your desired audience. Your videos will auto-play muted on scroll, encouraging users to tap or click to open the tweet and watch. Twitter will show your ad as a "Video Card" that consists of your ad copy (max. 140 characters), a video, a video title (max. 70 characters), and a video description (max. 200 characters). You pay for video views, which Twitter defines as follows:

"A view occurs when a video is at least 50% in-view on the user's device and has been watched for at least 2 seconds, or the user clicks to watch the video in fullscreen."

Promoted tweet with video

Grow your followers

If you want to promote your Twitter account and grow your follower base, this is the ad type for you. Twitter suggests to your target audience that they follow your account, and also indicates whether any of their followers follow your account. These ads show up in the user feed and in the "Who to follow" sidebar on Desktop. You pay for every follower the ad generates.

Promoted account in sidebar   **Promoted account in feed**

Website visits

Drive your audience to your website using this campaign type. Twitter will display your message in a "Website Card" that consists of your ad copy (max. 116 characters), an image and a website title/description (max. 70 characters). You will pay for website link clicks.

Twitter:

Website conversions

This ad type makes use of the "Website Card" shown above, but optimizes campaigns for conversions such as purchases or downloads on your website. Advertisers have to integrate the Twitter website tag on their site, so Twitter can track conversion. User data about interests and intent helps Twitter optimize the campaign delivery. Although the objective is conversion, you still pay for website link clicks.

App installs and re-engagements

If your campaign objective is to generate downloads of your mobile app or motivate people to open it again, this could be a great ad type for you. This promoted tweet is shown as an "App Card" which consists of an ad copy (116 characters), an image, the app name, price and rating (pulled from the app store), and a call to action button. You can choose to either pay for app link clicks or app installs.

Lead generation

With the lead generation campaign type, you can create promoted tweets that aim to collect the user's email address, so you can follow up with a newsletter or offer. The Lead Generation Card includes your ad copy (116 characters), a Call to Action button (20 characters), a short description (50 characters) and an image. If a user clicks the Call to Action button, Twitter will submit the name and email associated with the user's Twitter account and show a customizable message (100 characters). You pay for the number of leads generated.

Twitter:

What targeting options does Twitter offer?

Twitter offers the following nine targeting options that you can combine as needed:

Location: Target users by country, state, region, metro area, or ZIP code.

Gender: You can target only male or only female users or both. Twitter infers genders from information users share as they use Twitter, e.g., their profile names.

Languages: By default, Twitter delivers campaigns to all languages, so make sure to target only people who understand your message.

Devices, Platforms and Carriers: Target users who use specific mobile devices (e.g. iOS, Android, Blackberry) and mobile phone carriers (e.g. AT&T, Verizon) to access Twitter. You can also target users based on when they first used Twitter on a new device or carrier.

Interest: Target users based on 25 interest categories that expand into 350 subtopics, from Automotive to Travel. Twitter identifies user interests based on what content users engage with and what usernames they follow.

Followers: Provide Twitter with a list of usernames and your ad will reach users who have similar interests as those who follow any of the accounts you have listed.

Keyword: Reach users based on the keywords of their search queries, recent Tweets, and Tweets they recently engaged with. For each keyword, you can define whether you want to target users with exact keyword matching, broad matching (i.e., Twitter will also target related keywords) or negative matching (i.e., Twitter won't target users who match for this keyword).

Behavior: To target users based on their online and offline behavior (e.g., product or shopping preferences), Twitter utilizes user data that third-party data providers have shared with them.

Tailored Audiences: With tailored audiences, you can target existing customers, leads or website visitors. To do this, you have to upload a list of emails, Twitter IDs or mobile advertising IDs. Alternatively, you can put a code snippet on your website so Twitter can identify your website visitors. You can either focus a campaign on a tailored audience, or exclude the tailored audience if you prefer to reach only new prospects.

Twitter:

What is the minimum budget to advertise on Twitter?

Twitter requires you to set up a maximum daily budget for your campaigns, after which Twitter will stop distributing your ad. Optionally, you can also set a maximum budget for the duration of the whole campaign. The cost of an action (defined by campaign type, as explained earlier) depends on how much other advertisers, who compete with you for the same audience, bid. Unlike Facebook and Instagram, Twitter does not ask you to commit a minimum budget.

How to get started

To get started you need an active Twitter account. Go to Twitter Ads and you will be prompted with a screen where you select your campaign objective. These objectives match the ones we have discussed above.

Pinterest:

About Pinterest

Photo and video sharing site Pinterest lets users upload, save, sort, and organize images and videos, called pins, in personal and collaborative collections, called boards. The platform now reports 150 million monthly active users, who contribute to what the Pinterest CEO calls the "Catalogue of Ideas".

Many businesses, especially in the fashion, art or interior design space, have successfully used Pinterest to promote their products organically and have developed a following which engages with their content. Promoted Pins are Pinterest's native advertising format – they look and behave the same way as regular Pins, but advertisers can pay to have them seen by more users.

What ad types does Pinterest offer?

Currently, Pinterest only offers one advertising type to all businesses in the US, Canada, and the UK: The Promoted Pin. The company is also testing a Pin in which you can directly buy the product you see (Buyable Pin), but this feature is currently only available to a limited audience.

Promoted Pins are inserted into a user's feed and search results.They look exactly like regular Pins, but are marked as "Promoted Pins".

You can buy Promoted Pins optimized for three different campaign objectives: Awareness, Engagement, and Traffic.

Awareness campaigns

Awareness campaigns are the right choice if your main objective is to get your brand or product exposed to as many people in your target audience as possible. A lot of people use Pinterest to discover new ideas and get inspiration without a concrete plan in mind. Awareness campaigns get optimized for reach, not for engagement, and you will pay based on the number of impressions your Pins generate.

Pinterest:

Engagement campaigns

If you choose an engagement campaign, Pinterest will optimize the delivery of your Pins so they reach people who could be interested in saving or repinning them. These campaigns target people who are in the 'intent' stage and who are actively looking for solutions to their problems or ideas for their projects. This is also the right campaign type if your objective is to build a bigger following on Pinterest. You will be charged for engagement (close-ups, repins or clicks), not for impressions. Note that this campaign type won't direct users to your landing page. To do this, choose traffic campaigns.

Traffic campaigns

Traffic campaigns are designed to drive Pinterest users to an advertiser's landing page. So, if your objective is to target people who have completed the inspiration and planning phase and are ready to act (or buy), choose this campaign type. This is the only campaign type that will include a link to your landing page in the Promoted Pin. You will be charged for every link click.

What targeting options does Pinterest offer?

Pinterest offers a variety of targeting options that you can combine to build a specific audience:

Location: Target any combination of users from the US, Canada, and the UK, at the country level or at the metro level.

Languages: Target users who speak specific languages

Gender: Target users based on their gender

Devices: Target users based on the specific device they use to access Pinterest.

Keywords: Target users who search for a specific keyword (which must be relevant for your ad).

Interests: Target users based on other Pins they have saved and engaged with.

Audience: Target: people who have visited your website (you have to embed a Pinterest tag in the code of your site); existing customers or leads (you have to upload a list of email addresses); an audience that has engaged with Pins that link to your website; or an 'act-alike audience' that behaves similarly to your existing audience (you need to provide a list with at least 100 email addresses of customers who are also Pinterest users).

Pinterest:

What is the minimum budget to advertise on Pinterest?

Once you have set up a campaign and entered your bid for a specific audience you target, Pinterest will give you some guidance on whether your bid seems promising or not. Only awareness campaigns require a minimum budget; the other two campaign types do not require a minimum bid. Have a look at the table below to understand how you may be charged:

Advertising objective:	What your maximum bid means:
Awareness	Your bid is the maximum you are willing to pay for every 1,000 people (CPM) who see your Promoted Pin. The minimum you can bid is $5.
Engagement	Your bid is the maximum you are willing to pay when a user engages with a Promoted Pin, i.e. close-ups, repins and click-throughs (Cost Per Engagement, CPE). Important: if a user close-ups, repins and clicks through on your Pin, you will be charged for each of these actions.
Traffic	Your bid is the maximum you are willing to pay for each click a person makes on your Promoted Pin to visit your website (CPC).

How to get started

To get started, you need a Pinterest business accoun. You can also convert your existing account into a business account. After you have registered your business account, you can start running ads.

Snapchat:

About Snapchat

Snapchat started out as visual instant messaging service and has now evolved into a combination of a multimedia messaging and content platform. Snapchat now has more than 200 million monthly active users, many of them Millennials. They exchange snaps and stories with their friends and access the media content provided by editorial partners.

Since 2015 advertisers can reach Snapchat's users through different ad placements and sponsorships. The majority of advertising offerings is currently only available to bigger advertisers with considerable budgets. But one ad type, the On-Demand Geofilter, is bookable through self-service.

What ad types does Snapchat offer?

Most of Snapchat's advertising options are targeted at large brands and companies, and can't be booked through a self-service platform like the other options we have seen so far. Only Sponsored Geofilters are available through self-service, so keep that in mind when evaluating advertising channels.

Snapchat Discover

It's not officially listed on the website, but brands can take over a publisher's channel in the Discover section of the app for about $50,000 a day. If you want to sponsor a Live Story (also a feature in the Discovery section), you can expect to pay about $250,000.

Sponsored Lenses

Sponsored Lenses are a very interactive format in which users engage with promotional elements that overlay a video user's film of her/himself. Snapchat reports that the average user plays for 20 seconds with a Sponsored Lens, which can really help a brand drive awareness. Taco Bell's Sponsored Lens received over 224 million views. But high engagement comes with a high price tag: Sponsored Lenses can cost $500,000 or more – per day.

Snapchat:

Snap Ads

Snap Ads are 10-second vertical mobile video ads with the option to swipe up for more related content, such as another video, article, ad or mobile website. Snapchat says that five times more users swipe up on Snap Ads than click through on ads on comparable platforms. Pricing for Snap Ads depends on the details of the campaign, but can be as low as $1,000. Currently Snap Ads can only be booked through Snapchat's Partners.

Sponsored Geofilters

This is the only advertising option you can book yourself online and with a small budget. Geofilters, however, are a very specific ad type that only suits some campaign objectives. Geofilters are pre-designed overlays such as frames, logos, images or text elements that Snapchat users can use to decorate their snaps if they are in a certain location. Companies and brands can purchase Geofilters for a
specific location (between 20,000 and 5,000,000 square feet) to promote their product, services or event.

Also, big brands like Starbucks or McDonald's make use of Sponsored Geofilters targeting
the locations of their stores. This way customers are encouraged to share their experience in a playful way.

Snapchat:

If your objective is to promote a store in a mall, a party on campus, a booth at a conference, or anything else that is of interest to Snapchat users in a specific location, Geofilters could be an interesting choice for you. You can also use Geofilters to create some entertainment for your friends or guests at a wedding, birthday or any other personal occasion. But if you want to target users in a whole city or country, or by specific interests or behaviors, this is probably not the right choice for you.

How much do Sponsored Geofilters cost?

The price of a Geofilter depends on the dates, times and the area size (measured in square feet) of your Geofilter. Pricing begins at $5 for a Geofilter covering a small area during a short period of time, but Snapchat will show you an exact quote once you have entered this information in their booking platform.

How to get started

Go to https://www.snapchat.com/geofilters and log in with your Snapchat account information. The Geofilter creation tool walks you through the design process, helping you with customizable templates. Alternatively, design your personal Geofilter in your favorite image editing software (e.g., Adobe Photoshop) and upload your file. Choose the dates (min. 1 hour, max. 30 days) and define the location of your Geofilter (currently only the US, UK and Canada): Enter the address closest to the area you want to advertise and draw a fence around your selected area. Your area must be between 20,000 and 5,000,000 square feet. Snapchat then quotes you a price and you can submit your order for approval. If you have any questions, have a look at the related section on the Snapchat Support site.

LinkedIn:

About LinkedIn

LinkedIn is the largest professional social network in the world with more than 460 million registered accounts. Of these, about 106 million users visit the site at least once a month. In addition to allowing users to connect with each other and search for business contacts, LinkedIn offers group features, company pages, and job listings. They also have a publishing platform on which invited thought leaders, influencers, and all other registered users can publish posts.

From an advertising standpoint, LinkedIn can be a great platform for two purposes: To promote employers, their jobs and stories, and to advertise products and services that are of interest to a professional audience.

What ad types does LinkedIn offer?

LinkedIn offers two types of ads – Sponsored Content and Text Ads. These ad types can be booked via LinkedIn's self-service platform, called Campaign Manager. In addition, larger advertisers can book display ads and promotional messages, called Sponsored InMail, via the LinkedIn Ad Sales team.

Sponsored Content

LinkedIn's Sponsored Content Ad allows you to publish a promotional update on users' newsfeeds, alongside all the updates from their regular connections. The update is marked as 'Sponsored,' but other than that it looks and behaves exactly like a normal update. Your update can include an image, video, infographic, PDF, SlideShare or link to a blog post or landing page.

To set up a Sponsored Content Ad, you need to have access to a Company Page or a Showcase Page, or create a new one. Your content will be shared in the name of this company or brand. With a click on the user name or icon, people can visit the respective page and follow your updates. Your Sponsored Content Ad can either promote an existing update from your page or an update you create specifically for your campaign. LinkedIn gives you various targeting options to reach your desired audience, which we will cover later.

LinkedIn:

Text Ads

LinkedIn Text Ads are traditional ads that appear in the right column of the desktop and in other locations on their website. A Text Ad consists of a small image (50x50 pixels), a short headline (25 characters), a description (75 characters) and a link to your landing page or LinkedIn Company Page.

Ads You May Be Interested In

A 99% Employment Rate
Get recruited by all of the Big 4 and middle-market accounting firms. ›

Want to be a boss?
Supercharge your leadership skills with an MBA from top CEO Jack Welch.

Simple Story Videos
We add strategy to your story to create an impactful video. 1-877-513-2422.

LinkedIn Text Ad

What targeting options does LinkedIn offer?
LinkedIn lets you target users based on their demographics, education, professional experience, and group memberships:

Demographics: Target users by age, gender and location.
Education: Target users by schools, degrees and field of study.
Experience: Target users by job function and title, seniority, skills, company name, company industry and company size.
Groups: Target users by the groups they belong to on LinkedIn.

What is the minimum budget to advertise on LinkedIn?
You can set up your Sponsored Content and Text Ad campaigns both as a click (CPC) or impression (CPM) based campaigns. The minimum daily budget for both ad types is $10.

With both campaign types, the LinkedIn Campaign Manager will show you a suggested bid range based on what other advertisers are bidding for the same audience. The minimum CPC or CPM bid for Text Ads is $2. For Sponsored Content, the minimum bid depends on your target audience.

How to get started
To get started, access LinkedIn's Campaign Manager by logging in and then click on "Create Ad". This will present you with a screen where you can select your ad type. LinkedIn will then walk you through the ad creation, targeting and budgeting process.

Become a Divibe Tech Client! :

About Divibe Tech

We are a Growth Hacking Marketing Company. Our greatest reward is the praise we get from clients after they see their bottom line increase (yeah, that's a little cheesy, but it's true). But we also love the praise that comes from others. We are constantly adjusting and re-evaluating our internet marketing services to fit the specific needs, goals and expectations of each company. Well-researched and well-executed campaigns do deliver results over time. But sometimes, even we are surprised by the numbers that sites can achieve with our help. Every business is different, and the challenges our clients face evolve as they change and grow. We are proud to be the chosen partner of many iconic brands but also for hundreds of small to medium-sized businesses as well. We have loads of experience working with different types of businesses in almost every major industry. What this means for you is that whatever your situation, there's a good chance we already have experience in your industry or type of business, or at least with something very similar.

Our Vision

Through our growth hacking strategies we want to help our economy and help hundreds of businesses in many different industries such as Dentists, Plumbers, Veterinarians, Home Builders, Software Companies, Ecommerce companies etc. We want to help you create your legacy. Run the marathon, don't sprint.

Meet Laura Egocheaga

As a thought leader in her field Laura Egocheaga is a web developer, designer, SEO specialist, growth hacker and author. Born in Lima, Peru she immigrated to the United States when she was 4 years old and has lived in Tampa, Florida ever since. Laura was introduced to entrepreneurship her Junior year of High School where she made $20,000 in just 6 months from affiliate marketing. From there she finished school and went to college to only drop out. She taught herself how to code and through experience, learned all the skills she takes advantage of today. Laura went from working for the biggest market research and marketing agency in the world to owning her own agency that focuses on small business growth because she understands that small businesses at the backbone to our economy

Contact us: DivibeTech.com , Call Us @ (813)817-7011
All Social Media: @LauraEgocheaga ; @DivibeTech

Made in the USA
Monee, IL
11 October 2021

79814926R00017